calling home

PRAISE SONGS AND INCANTATIONS

Bilingual Press/Editorial Bilingüe

CANTO COSAS

Address

Bilingual Press
Hispanic Research Center
Arizona State University
PO Box 875303
Tempe, Arizona 85287-5303
(480) 965-3867

NAOMI AYALA

calling home

PRAISE SONGS AND INCANTATIONS

Bilingual Press/Editorial Bilingüe
TEMPE, ARIZONA

Library of Congress Cataloging-in-Publication Data

Ayala, Naomi, 1964-
[Poems. Selections]
Calling home : praise songs and incantations / Naomi Ayala.
pages cm. — (Canto Cosas)
Poems.
ISBN 978-1-931010-89-4 (alk. paper)
I. Title.
PS3551.Y23C35 2013
811'.54—dc23

2013011031

PRINTED IN THE UNITED STATES OF AMERICA

Front cover art Camino a Elegua *(2010) by Lázaro Batista*
Cover and interior design by John Wincek

Permissions and source acknowledgments are on p. 83.

CANTO COSAS

This poetry series, which was initially supported by awards from the National Endowment for the Arts and the Arizona Commission on the Arts, is designed to give further exposure to Latina and Latino poets who have achieved a significant level of critical recognition through individual chapbooks and publication in periodicals or anthologies or both, but who in most cases have not had their own books of poetry published. Under the watchful eye of series editor, poet, and small press publisher Francisco Aragón, the books in Canto Cosas aim to reflect the aesthetic diversity in American poetry. There are no restrictions on ethnicity, nationality, philosophy, ideology, or language; we will simply continue our commitment to producing high-quality poetry. The books in this series will also feature introductions by more established voices in the field.

For my father,
Peter Dolores Ayala Sepúlveda,
and my brother,
Reynaldo Ayala Santiago

CONTENTS

Acknowledgments xi
Foreword: *Every Memory an Orisha,* Lorna Dee Cervantes 1

..... **5**

In the Beginning 7
Winter 8
For Resentment 9
Declaración Número Sabe-Quién for a Telling-Off 10
Brujo No. 7, Against the Noise of Urban Development 11
Trasnocharse 13
Brujo No. 39, for Ease 14
Sanación No. 11, Mt. Rainier 15
For Reverence 16
Joined 17
No. 13, for Remembering 19
Lineage 21

..... **23**

Taíno Is in Me 25
Abuela 26
Puerto Rico 27

Vieques 28
Migration 29
Coño 31
Declaración in the Time of the Chameleon 32
For Light 33
Benediction 34
Chucho 35
Golden Chopsticks 36
Tiene que ser 37
Two Tamales 38
Cántaro 39
For the City 40
Because She Asked 41
Bridge Across the Pond 42
Tenderfoot 43
Carmen Inés Goes to the Botánica 44
Penance 45
Music Man 46
One Season 47
Ring 51

53

For Remembrance 55
Rock Creek 56
Turtle Country 57
Stone Song 58
Sanación de Manuel Santos 59

Night, Leaving North 60
Consejo No. 13, Given by an Otherwise Ill-Willed Papi Chulo Pueblo Man, a Tewa, Who Cared About Prayers 61
Security Shift 62
Porcupine 63
Lontananza 64
Manuel Plays Bizet's Andante, Symphony in C 65
Clean Slate 66
Hallway, Cooperative High School 67
For Deliverance 68
Brujo No. 1 for the Papi Chulo Who Must Go 69
Sanación, Barrio 71
Declaración No. 999 for Harmony 72
Brujo No. 28 for Drawing Your Ancestors 73
Eyes Looking 74
Manifesto 76

Notes 77
Permissions and Source Acknowledgments 83

ACKNOWLEDGMENTS

For their ability to place love at the center of all things, their ingeniousness, and their determination to thrive culturally, I am grateful to my family.

Many thanks to the DC Commission on the Arts for an artist fellowship that made much of the work for this book possible.

My thanks also to Robert Bradley Farr Jr. for help editing many of the poems in this manuscript.

For their personal and professional camaraderie, *cariñitos* and deepest gratitude to Karen Lapuk, Roberto Solórzano, O.C. Heaton, E. Ethelbert Miller, Gina Robles-Villalba, Ernesto Torres Almodóvar, Laura Urioste, the Tayac family and the Piscataway Nation, José Carlos Merino, Lázaro Batista, Ariana Quiñones and Sami Miranda, Manuel Cabrera Santos, Bob Russell, Sunil Freeman, Kevin Bowen, Francisco Aragón, Nora Comstock and *Las Comadres para las Américas*, Betsy VanWaganen, Enrique Suárez, James C. Boone, and Jerrold Boone.

EVERY MEMORY AN ORISHA

Lorna Dee Cervantes

Naomi Ayala's poetry is an intricate tapestry in which images of contemporary life are interwoven with the wisdom of the ancient Yoruba religion and related Borinquen traditions.

Here are praise songs and incantations in which ". . . every memory is an Orisha"; here the discovered, the covered up, the recovered, and the rediscovered transform every poem into a reconquest of spirit and an exhibition of mastery.

No matter the subject, Naomi Ayala has come of age as a poet. Moving effortlessly from world to world, strategy to strategy, she skips across the known and named obstacles of racial, cultural, sexual, class, and linguistic identities as surely as a well-aimed stone skims across a swollen river to arrive at a place where many worlds are possible.

Two Tamales

. . . I would make you a chipotle sauce
with songs of back home.
Use the cilantro of my words
to have a little green to chew on.
Before the corn husks dry again
I would make you a little love
in the shape of a flower constantly blooming.
These hands I keep for myself, though.
They belong to the world now.
Everything else you can have—
my pillow, my jug of water, this poem,
the love I'll have for your eyes

when they look at me
past the self I am in front of them
looking past the both of us.

Here you will discover the lives you may never have known existed—those Others defined at last by what they do rather than by being told what they are by someone with the authority to do so.

Brujo No. 28 for Drawing Your Ancestors

Face it. This here's about loss
and regaining what's been lost.
Call your spirit back.
What is the birthing song you need?
The secret vow?
If your day is a drum, then drum.
The rest is about dancing.

Ayala's incantations express the amulets of lives tossed back into being by presenting us with the "minute particulars," as Blake said, or, as William Carlos Williams (with the Borinqueña mother) put it, "no ideas but in things."

Herein lie the lives of those who "keep a small house." Peer into the dimmed lives lived outside by those "who think only white is for purification." Here are the final reports from those who "went missing from policed appearances" and a counting of coup for those who don't count except as brazos or as corpses.

Turtle Country

The wind pulls city dust
into the masculine
corners of eyes,
all at once lifting
the hems of skirts
without warning,
and I remember him,

without October sallow,
like this land that is his country
risen on turtle's back.

Ayala does the best that poetry can do. She is the poet to whom things speak, no matter how they are called. The poem is not subjected to the poet's will; instead it emerges from the reading consciousness like the young deer in the poem "Rock Creek" climbs "down the darkening hills." These poems bring wakefulness to the reader. They remind me of who I am and what I am not.

Much as in the poetry of Mary Oliver, this is a poetry that "binds me to a world / of human things," even if those bindings are "just deer / going to water." As in the best of e.e. cummings, this is a poetry that won't do as it's told, a "poetry glad and big / . . . / loud and strong" ("Manifesto"), as in the voice of the coquí refusing to go extinct.

Read and discover Ayala's incantations, Taíno spells of land and tongue, the lost stews and simmering culture as real as the single onion on an old woman's table. Here is a lodestone, a bodega, a place of worship and refuge, a house built of words called home. Simply put, *Calling Home* is the best book of poetry you'll read in a long time, by a Latina or any other.

Within these pages you will discover América, and call it home.

San Francisco, CA
December 7, 2011

An infinite multiplicity of becomings variously colored, so to speak, passes before our eyes: we manage so that we see only differences of color, that is to say, differences of state, beneath which there is supposed to flow, hidden from our view, a becoming always and everywhere the same, invariably colorless.

HENRI-LOUIS BERGSON,
L'Évolution créatrice

IN THE BEGINNING

There was the word.
And the word was sound
that ran through the Earth
like water and covered
the land of your body.
It flooded your eyes, flowered
in the pit of your hands.
It stirred in your ribs
and cooled in your breast.
It fired your throat,
parted your lips for a crow,
and I heard the news
and came running.
O sweet song, sweet breath.
In me gathered a thousand waves
calling home out of the darkness.

WINTER

There's a gulf between me and God.
I fill it with angry fish
whose backs catch the sun.
I call across and listen for the wind,
watch tall snowdrifts
wrap around the cadaver boughs of trees.
When the gulf freezes over
I sing out—sometimes to myself,
sometimes to the water beneath the ice.
There is always water waiting to be called back—
a whole world moving beneath the ice—
even in my heart,
weighed with the tundra of forgetting.

FOR RESENTMENT

In the year you were fifty-three
you had wanted to believe
in a miracle of cloud—
something you could come through
clean,

kiss
the sacredness of rain
on the mouth,

but the wind bared you
to bone first.

He who knows all things
beat you like a drum

and you had to stop,
and you had to listen.

DECLARACIÓN NÚMERO SABE-QUIÉN FOR A TELLING-OFF

These are my screams
whipping the fence posts.
When will you discern
between love song and grinding glass?

You cannot even
tell your own story.
It is void of you.

And what would you have
me do with it anyway?

Couldn't catch the Metro
across town with it,
pull down a star
from the 19th Street marquee.

Couldn't put it between my breasts
and sleep with it at night.
Couldn't go down on it.

BRUJO NO. 7, AGAINST THE NOISE OF URBAN DEVELOPMENT

Buildings go up and come down.
Two-story garage, converted.
No real pa'lante in this.
Daily drill bits to concrete.
The side-swoon of cranes.

My name is Lucky 7
who survived migration.
Hail progress and its numbers.
Profit increment dependency.
All sing to piggy-back economics,
the stability of greed.

I am Lucky 7, embodied brujo
who shrieks outside the kitchen window
at three years of construction
that will populate the backyard alley,
highway connector of rats, with yuppies.
I peer out my window
morning coffee in hand.

All hail the dress code,
the Pavlovian personae,
uncamouflaged.

I am seven bachatas, merengues,
seven pots beaten with a spoon,
seven drums from seven nations
at seven thousand feet.

Seven toilets flushing and hammers nailing.
Seven poets singing
in the red light night.
Seven security alarm systems
protecting heavy machinery
till the all too early
breakfast of noise
gets you up and out.

I am Lucky 7, losing my teeth,
dreaming in tongues.
The spells I cast for you
I wrap in shawls
handed down to me by old women
who knew God went missing
the day we could
no longer end where we begin.

TRASNOCHARSE

This word, the opposite of sleep,
meaning to pierce the night through.

While linen breathes the body's scent
under the cold moon,
the perfectly linear streets
pretend to have their heads put down.

Drug, balm, purgative
to relieve the mind from lack,
the belly from regret,
shapeshift longing.

How can I squeeze and shape
these angry pillows
into an intelligent winding
of arms around my body,
remember myself sleeping,
and so give up, go in?

BRUJO NO. 39, FOR EASE

I want a dark brown hat,
crow feathers on the right side.
I want to watch the reflections
of passersby in Gary Taylor's Fine Arts
and Framing storefront window,
see how they look against blue.

I want shoes that say Open 24-7 in rhinestone script
so I can remember who I am,
catch a rainy season, arrive sopping wet
somewhere.

I'm going to quit pain today,
look away from his cave-brown eyes,
not let his memory be
my bedside lamp

on claustrophobic Tuesdays at three a.m.,
reaching for kisses in unhealed wounds
that speak in their tongues of silence
the lapping flame that knows us all.

I will unearth my shadows
from their paved-over tombs,
dance with their frail skeletons,
call them by name in the eye,

see my reflection
and let go with ease.

I want a natural break—
un-human,
starlike.

SANACIÓN NO. 11, MT. RAINIER

How to tell you that
even Tahoma retreats from me a little.
I am a stubborn woman
reinventing geographies
where your hands are birds
that wake me.

And exactly because of you
this note will fly
into the Tahoma wind
without your knowing.
Tahoma will bring me to her lap.
I'll learn to be a mountain.

FOR REVERENCE

Sleepless drunks stumble
from bodega glass mouths,
an hour before bank closes.

One foot of snow on the ground;
gloved, loose-change hand.

Children trampoline from a mattress
in the Kenyon Street alleyway.

The trees are frozen.
Long, bony fingers shake up
telephone wire web.

A flock of crows
puts out the pale dusk sky,
scatters a barn owl into flight,

while the slowly darkening rooftops
sing of Baghdad, poke at the sky

without lights,
deadly fireworks.

And day meets night,
a small breath in the cold air.

JOINED

for Abigail

Rain—
dagger rain of the gods,
unstoppable deluge,

three weeks after she quit crack,
rubbing palm against brow
like there was blood on it,
blood like we've never
seen together.

Child-blood.
Grow-blood.

Willful rain—
bury-me water
—down, down
on my still, black shoes,
on my guilty laces
lying through their perfect
crisscross road.

Sea-rain returning
to parched song
in tiny, thorny droplet blooms.

Unimaginable rain—
furious—when Abby reaches
for the hairline edge
of late-night dreams,

woman dreaming
blackbird ghosts.

Before the bus pulls up
to our side of the street, Abby
rubbing palm against brow now,
finds me laughing
when I want to cry,
dancing
like it was Saturday night,
a half pint of Wild Turkey
between us—

dancing, like nothing
was holding us in place,
like there was no rain at all.

NO. 13, FOR REMEMBERING

Two blocks away
where yellow cabs
zip by without stopping
and the prostitute with the skinny legs
asks for a cigarette
from under her giant
black umbrella,

in the corner's rain
where some children
are dangerous,
can tell our future
and bet on broken love
between the dreams,

I don't know where my hands begin
and my heart ends.

Oak trees line the sidewalk,
small birds carry spring twigs
above fast-food waste,
and the bold races of rats,
like ghosts of a lost memory,
point to the day of the week.

I don't know where the face of change
is not my own face.

A cold wind picks up.
A man abandons himself
to a tambourine and harmonica—

not praising, not denouncing,
only leaving this place with this sound.

I don't know where we will
end up and begin
but I want to note
that we have been here,
that we too were invisible
and we too were seen.

LINEAGE

You polished their floors and shined their windows
blessing the light that clothed your body,
fixed roofs and hung from scaffolds,
nursed their children like your own,
taught them at schools, prayed over them,
kept the searing god of heat at bay in kitchens.

You were the five-and-dime beauty queen,
the jeans and tee shirt looker,
taught everyone how to pronounce your name,
learned to build their houses till, bent back,
you could not build your own.

You were the good people,
the nice island, dark brown country folk,
the symbol of work ethic,
envy of this country's unemployed
at minimum wage and below.

You straightened your hair, permed it,
tried to bleach yourself clean, polish your accent,
even learned Spanish all over again,

changed your name and changed it back
till it was winter in your body and the winds came—
love's lineage sweeping you with song.

So beautiful, so yourself, you stand—
my heart, too small for the beauty of your transgressions,
your survivals, your becomings.

¿Y encuentras en la calavera

tu estirpe a hueso condenada?

PABLO NERUDA,
El libro de las preguntas

TAÍNO IS IN ME

I know simple things. I can testify I heard the bones
of my people shift beneath the earth,
on the corner of 18th and Columbia,
by the man who Cubanized an *Oye, oye m'ijo*—
while the US launched a bomb
and a pigeon swooped down like a different bird.
I stood still and my pores were ears when a wind came.
Early chill of August.
Unspeakable Metro bus fuel.
Ambulance siren backlash heart.
The bones of my people shift below
in the body of the Earth which is my body.
I know why the sun gives us dreams
rising up on the horizon line,
between left foot and right foot in the morning,
how it enters a woman,
the moon's counsel still burning in our ears.
I hear a güiro. I hear a cuatro. I hear a drum.
I carry trees and rock and sky and river-canoe in my soul
and bones, bones intact enough to hurt.

ABUELA

At the Women's Jingle Dress dance
she points to my cheekbones,
asks am I Native American.
Taíno, I say, afraid someone
might be listening.
Sometimes I hide my smile
in the oceans of white faces.
They might not know that,
like you, I am old on the Earth.
I think of you today, our ancestors,
and want to walk off
into these green fields of September—
lost forever from the cities,
sing to the sun.
You live in me in the form of a river,
this river that's ours,
that gives our love shape.

PUERTO RICO

They named you *rich port.*
Now your resources burn away.

Yet the corn smiles,
pineapple crowns stretch up to the sky,
the cane is still sweet,
though a giant lives beneath them.

I have named her
Woman Who Knows All Who Walk Through.
She can cough fire,
sing her enemies to sleep.

I have named this sleep
Hole in the Sky.
That dreamtime place of no wind,
with its dim suns,
maimed hands,
screams,
gunfire,
wild dogs—

though flowers bloom beneath them
anyway.

I have named these flowers
New Children Who Heal Up the Past.
They will be related to my own.
We will grow into the earth like rain.

VIEQUES

Because a crop of sleeping hand grenades maim
hands that wrestled the sacrifice of cane,
tobacco leaf and coffee—
squeezing 500 ungodly years
into a crown of spiny blooms at the brow—
fishing people now take to sea
in tiny boats to swallow synthetic lightning.

Men with souls
locked and polished like machine guns
move in at suppertime,
set up training camps, bomb storehouses,
drive their gleaming future
into earth womb and swollen sea.

Because in the hills, as on the coast,
beneath a quickening of sorties,
jíbaro dreams rise through America's blood wail—

and two stones spark a flame
and the crickets are rebellious
and the birds know
and the sea knows
and cows stir in the pastures
and the bones of our dead sing,

songs of iron-will
drive love into the coastline
through 500 years and one hundred to come—
love that will swallow lightning
only to cough up winged fists,
restore the soul of the dead to the living,
fish to water, lightning to sky.

MIGRATION

Uan
She dreamt up the little havens.

Tu
It was cold, like the nightmare scythe
falling y mucho, mucho más.

Tri
No refuge—albergue
—only the heart
inside the heart
where there was so much of everything
disposable*desechable*disposable*desechable*,

and always,
of course, war.
Pero tú sabes,
de afueritas,
in someone else's yard.

For
Nipa.
The tírame-jálame of the city.

Fai
Se enseña inglés.
Se habla español.
ESL free come Wednesday
after the job cuts
down, the children, the house—
aspira.
Aspira que te aspira to perspire.

Sics

Two tongues now
and such a shortage of words.
Tú sabes,
aún se atora la lengua.

COÑO

I want to speak,
the woman said to the guard.
Yes, said the guard,
but aquí no se habla español.

Go on, though.
I have my dictionary.
How do you spell that, please?

Nauseated, defiantly polite,
Spanglish staggering along,
María gunned her *¡Coño!*

I'm sorry, said the guard.
No such word here.

Doña María, fixing to draw
deliver-me-Lord paws
to the guard's face,
imagined the wide marks
and the screeching.

But you can't draw blood
from rocks
or walls.
¡Mierda!

DECLARACIÓN IN THE TIME OF THE CHAMELEON

Turning loose
with my green dreaming,
they say I slip past gatekeepers
to trace out stories that scratch
behind the night's stained walls
till you are one who hears.
I wear my listening,
the eye of the unsuspecting.
I take my becomings into my flank.
I move fast, invisibly.
I am not a translation, a lie.

FOR LIGHT

Wielding her staff,
a mop I could not push forward,
she made the sun rise inside her. Titi Luz—
mother of Nilda, Esquimalito,
wife of Vitín—who lived in the city, Río Piedras,
carried a bucket of Pine Sol water
for the finished concrete floors of the local school
as if she had lifted it from a river full of gold.

A river I've swum in till dusk,
she waving from the bank across,
till we were both golden.

All grown, I would clean houses
in the nice part of town,
cursing my cracked hands,
wiping myself clean inside.

A friend who cleaned with me sometimes
would quiet me down with her eyes,
as if to say women who need work
can't be that proud, when the most
well-kept lady, who was not a lady,
would point to the bagful of cans in the garage
waiting for their nickel deposits
she'd saved for us instead of a tip.

And I prayed to make it,
prayed to my Titi Luz,
the woman the sun
bowed down on like maíz—
Titi Luz, who loved me.

BENEDICTION

Loíza at dusk. Burnt sienna hands
cupping almond tree leaves.
The smell of alcapurrias
from the roadside cooking drums.
The perfection of sky.
Potato sacks filled with mangoes.
Crossing a boarded
bridge over the river.
How the river rose
into a giant with arms and legs
and angry mouth
during hurricane season.
How I thought God, Huracán,
was the water, lived in its body,
in the drums
beat by the cane fields
and hollow shacks,
lived in the coconut
shell masks of her fiestas,
where it calls to me still.

CHUCHO

On the corner of Blatchley and Grand
Chucho makes arepas
because it is Sunday
and far from Cuba, Puerto Rico, the Dominican Republic,
in a cacophony of Spanglish,
all the santos sing out
in their native tongues,
wide-open-mouthed, strong.
And every memory
is an Orisha
landing open-palmed on a drum,
void of sirens,
crowded buses,
machine shops and morgues,
though just as loud
moving in him,
in his body,
lifting his blessing
over his arepas,
above the Sunday corner,
Blatchley and Grand.
The bodega closing,
street folk dispersing.
The world brand new kind of open
for twenty-four hours
before Monday work.

chopsticks

GOLDEN CHOPSTICKS

I like coming here,
makes New Britain at lunchtime
my perfect city.
Speaking Spanish
with Chinese men
excites me—
my camarones en ajillo con tostones,
and such delicacies,
my juguito natural.

Call me crazy
but I've been so linguistically oppressed
I could speak Spanish
to telephone poles
if they could hear me in Spanish—
Mira, prieto and
Long time astanding, eh?

Every good-looking man
come past me
I want to call out to
¡Ay, Papi! Mira, papi,
cómo me torturas—
especially after lunch,
on Tuesdays,
in New Britain.

TIENE QUE SER . . .

It's got to be Goya. Adobo Goya.
Adobito del alma, the seasoning blend of life.
In my Thai cooking, Italian escapades,
in the simplest eggs,
all the pasteles of mami's kitchen,
the 24-hour pig marinades.
Winter time and spring,
in my asopao, my arroz con gandures,
first escort to cilantro, aguacate,
before all the sofritos of my life.

TWO TAMALES

I would give you everything I have, and today
that is a little bit of sun and two tamales.
I would make you a chipotle sauce
with songs of back home.
Use the cilantro of my words
to have a little green to chew on.
Before the corn husks dry again
I would make you a little love
in the shape of a flower constantly blooming.
These hands I keep for myself, though.
They belong to the world now.
Everything else you can have—
my pillow, my jug of water, this poem,
the love I'll have for your eyes
when they look at me
past the self I am in front of them
looking past the both of us.

CÁNTARO

Walking beside you and walking
the Earth's back.
Through the portal of morning
to touch you.
Past street-drone,
the way light sweeps.
Spirit of Thespis
on singing fingers,
the small of my back.
Walking my body to clayed earth
to draw my pitcherful of water.
Through dusk and softening,
past love's canicular brink.

FOR THE CITY

The sky fashions a suit of clouds
and before long
it's gala night on Euclid Street.
Through rain, 19 days in a row,
the for-sale signs of the economy,
we come to porch starlight, black and tans.
Near a window someone sleeps
as if this were an island,
as if the world
would cough up a hammock in April
for the weary,
the shunned, the broke.

BECAUSE SHE ASKED

for Rebecca

In the afternoon rains, even the branches of trees
seemed to fight the sky.
Days were ruled by drunkenness,
the longing in unmet eyes.
Those years of curlers for my long, straight hair
to impress the young men stopping by
for truyas at four a.m.
Glasses of pitorro, coquito, lifting, passing hands.
The smell of mondongo and pasteles
pressing the air back.
Sereno draping the hillside,
expert hands tuning guitars
before the far-reaching aguinaldos, the deep jíbaro ones
about real life for country folk—
en lontananza then and full of longing—
and such güiros tilled like the earth.
Perhaps we talk and sing and play so loud
the way we did back then
because anguish can steal your tongue any time of year.

BRIDGE ACROSS THE POND

All night, we have been
standing here,
swaying in the wind.
Do we go?
Or do we go?
Where is Maridys, who was just
stretched out like a bough,
losing today's breakfast
of arepas y café?
El viento está jodío,
but there will be winter ahead.
An hour ago,
a little piece of Puerto Rico
still dangled
from Inés's earrings—
fish scales
in the shape of birds
from the artisans
at the Parque de las Palomas.

TENDERFOOT

At American high school, when the cafeteria girls
pinned me to the walls for my lunch
and bus money, she walked
passed a hundred turned heads to find me.

We rode buses from school together,
walked mostly,
two miles from downtown to the projects,
down the middle of the street
with our books when we could.

She left me always at my door,
walked two more blocks to hers
after apologizing for hurrying to her brother,
who had sickle-cell, who never left the house.

Off in the distance, her Jheri curl
like spirals of seaweed disappearing in water.

We lived with the comfort we were around the bend,
would always see each other daily.
I remember her eyes, the light in them undimmed
by the call to always be tending.

I search through the genius of memory,
hands in my pockets, without her name.

CARMEN INÉS GOES TO THE BOTÁNICA

There had been so much talk in our neighborhood
about brujos and spiritual protection,
special oils to anoint offerings, the tempting
stillness of lopped flowers in clear water
to keep peace about one's house,

amulets and escapularios for days of no pay
and good luck with the numbers,
to cross ourselves against the dreaded
ay benditos of misfortune, that she,

summoned by desire, leapt for the male imán—
a lodestone for true love—all faith, did away
with the pullings of the church to preserve
her humanity, steal away from the cold
steel blue pane of winter,

and it was then that sex, born in her imagination,
consummated like a forecast of rainstorm
and heavy lightning charges,
took a mouth and fingers, hungry thighs and pelvis,
became the corrugated breaths
of hands meeting hands

and that out of herself came an unsplit song of longing,
slung at the world like a fish line.

PENANCE

There was always something wrong with her.
Her head and back ached—
a migraine, a bad period.
If it was hurricane season,
it was the wooden windows of her house it took.
The land made slaves of men and women
and she was one of them.
It kept the poor, poor.
Happiness was a lie she could stir in her soup,
mash with boiled plantain and pork crisps
and it still would not make a meal good.
The sky was always
too sunny for singing, too gray for tears.
And now God's glass eye had fallen to her lap.
Hadn't I seen it? This lie?
She was sure I was there when it happened.

MUSIC MAN

Plays the guitar five hours a day,
smokes something to dream up his life.

Pretends he'll only need one more day to get through.
Shrinks away into the rows of crumbling houses,
trash alive with a salsa we never heard.

It is true that mami never came for you
and papi hardly did.
The way the island never came back to you.

But home's come here looking in the shape of a song today.
I will keep her till you call.
Find a phone booth.

ONE SEASON

When she got old,
it was about angels and dolls.
Cherubs morphed
from white soap
and clay scent-dispensers
in her bathroom hearth
and its overflow
of lipsticks, perfumes, creams.
Dolls in their blonde,
auburn, and black hair.
Theirs was the wooden
trim of the ceiling.
Their eyes warned down at you
when you came into the house.

She was the shuffler of cards
in the back room,
seer of dissolutions,
small cracks in the party wall
dividing flesh from soul.

She boiled invented roots,
lied when she spoke in tongues,
took offerings of chicken eggs,
lawn mowing, and milk.

They always came back—
even for the pain,
bad news about work,
the cheating wife or husband

—addicted to the possibility
of miracles, money in the cards.

At 12 he was already smoking,
already working to help out
a family of 14.
When he got old,
it was about flowers.

A super's job
covered the rent.
He changed light bulbs for Yalies,
mopped halls and painted
walls whiter than they had ever been.
The building owner
bought him a snow blower once,
before the cancer,
when tendonitis and arthritis
set in, gave him free reign
of the green mote.

No recao allowed, though,
mint or cilantro
but every square foot
he turned into a complex
orchestration of color
the likes of which he never
saw in machine shops,
while putting up sheetrock

or kneeling to lay
carpet and tiles.

For himself he worked now
and for himself
the flowers, macho man
of our childhood
now given up drinking. The man
who never touched sugar,
now grown a sweet tooth
for strawberry ice cream.

When they were both young,
she was his sylph.
He put money on the table,
she says, drank hard,
soon lost his looks.

His scarred hands make their way
through the flowers
at Eastern Market,
miles off from where he lives now.
Some weeks ago
he took a split to the head,
falling from a 22-foot ladder.
He won't give up work, ever,
he says. He's got to earn his keep.

She doesn't clean anymore, she says,
hardly ever cooks

though still keeps up the parties—
last one in honor of Changó.
The good fortune seekers
come and clean up,
bring milk and eggs and mow.
It pays the bills, she says,
keeps the small house.

RING

Around the grave's cross—
bone white, chalklike—coffee cans
that gave up their brand colors
to sultry air, filled with sod and daisies.
Singing, I think I have swept death away.
I reach out to touch it and its dust stains my hand,
falls away to my island's breezes
near this part of the Atlantic.
But this is not a day for lullabies.
The cool wind reaches in here
where my lips cannot move.

Me sacaron como Apache de la llanura y del viento,
me arrojaron como Inca de la barca del silencio
pero vengo de la sombra, del pasado y del futuro.
Me sacaron de las nubes donde desnudé la lluvia,
me sacaron de los montes donde desnudé la tierra.
Pero vuelvo en español, en yoruba y en taíno,
regresando por los montes estrenando un rostro nuevo.
Me sacaron, me sacaron, pero vuelvo.

CÉSAR SÁNCHEZ BERAS,
"Areito por todos"

FOR REMEMBRANCE

I didn't come here in sweat.
I came here laughing.
Laughing, I built the world.
Singing, I blew life into cell, rock, bone.
Ask me why I'm silent.
I speak the unwinding
through which the wind blows.
Listen and you will remember me.
There are echoes everywhere.
Laugh back.

ROCK CREEK

All along the path
the trees are tired strangers.
I see my reflection in the brush.
Young deer climb down
the darkening hills,
the motion bringing
wakefulness to my limbs,
but the deer
are just deer
going to water.
Back along the path,
tiredness, like winter's call,
returns to me—
what binds me to the world
of human things.
I stretch my arms out from my body,
two moving boughs that disappear
into the dark.

TURTLE COUNTRY

The wind pulls city dust
into the masculine
corners of eyes,
all at once lifting
the hems of skirts
without warning,
and I remember him,
without October sallow,
like this land that is his country
risen on turtle's back.

STONE SONG

Stone of the mind
that hears me calling,
speaking stone,
standing stone,
sitting stone,
praying stone,
stone of the spark,
stone beneath
and stone above,
river stone,
moon stone,
stone of the serpent,
sacrifice stone,
stone of the city,
stone of hunger
and stone of filling soup,
cold stone,
quiet stone,
desert stone,
stone of tongues I know,
beyond the ego's fires.

SANACIÓN DE MANUEL SANTOS

Forgiving enmity, his throat let in the wings
of alphabets and reason,
and opening, opening, it closed,
and opening, opening, it opened.
And dream followed dream.
And speaking followed speaking.
And in himself, the hole—a forced
window—night, the wind.
Gone a darkness
from which darkness had come
and which the darkness took.

NIGHT, LEAVING NORTH

I don't want the rain to touch me,
these October leaves,
the impending pebble in my shoe,
shaky finger pointing south.

But south we go,
you and I,
with our winter blankets for a bed,
hands cupped to the sky

as if we'd been born
just for this,

twilight draping the city's eyes
and you, who stopped
your wandering in one breath
to call me from your likeness.

prayers

CONSEJO NO. 13, GIVEN BY AN OTHERWISE ILL-WILLED PAPI CHULO PUEBLO MAN, A TEWA, WHO CARED ABOUT PRAYERS

For goodness' sake, put it down,
he spat out, alarmed, as we edged along
the Lamont Street sidewalk after midnight.
Never do that again.
People's prayers
go up on the wings of birds.
Fallen feathers
are the answered ones
coming back to earth.
If you take that one, for example,
someone will not hear back.

SECURITY SHIFT

Dawn,
caught sleeping
inside the pickup.
Upside the head,
sleep-slap—
wake, dream, sputter.
Smoke
from the Peltier
teepee
meeting sky,
dawn blue.
Stripped bare
streets
before capitol
traffic.
Tiny lamplights,
dead and slowly dying.
The heart
skipping beats.
Prison
colder in November
than outside
White House dawn.
Waking in truck,
dead caught,
thinking on him.

PORCUPINE

Tell me again, she asks,
he shifting his pointed weight,
how does the porcupine get its quills?

He could not embrace the creatures
of the wood, he says, not a turtle
with its smooth shell,
and wandered far, curling inward
at the hurting wind.
And there. Barb, quill.

He holds a hand below her ear.
We are all born
with the thing to kill love, he says,
against our will.

But there must have been
real predators, she says.
There were.

He holds her head on his lap till dawn,
till words curl inside themselves
along the treeless road.

LONTANANZA

Above the flights of rats,
newborn leaves,
dogwood, magnolia.

I met you like this,
in another country,
far from all these winters,
the past calling
long into the night air.

I was free from war,
a young girl in summer dresses—
jealous, tentative.

You were a compass,
the languishing year,
loved me first.

Tonight tracers
light the sky in Iraq
and everything
that's horrible.
I wonder if you watch
from afar as I watch.

You who never could bear
what kept me awake at night.

andante

MANUEL PLAYS BIZET'S ANDANTE, SYMPHONY IN C

The day stretches into the eternal café,
the sure step of migrant
birds and the park, for once,
seems fenceless.
Even the reddening leaves
in their perpetual falling, endless.
Wild autumn grasses stand out
like a good name now,
an elegy in the small
marches of the noontime rush,
a quiet roadside pavilion.

CLEAN SLATE

for Jorge Farinacci

When you left, the afternoon
of the day you went missing
from policed appearances,

I shied into my flank,
walked crooked through Saturday,
passed the woods of Sunday walk
into the smog of Monday
with its harried crowds,

collected tiny air globules
of memory in a magic pocket
meant for rain and soft speaking.

Like in dreams—
when I've seen, lived something
I wake without—Friday came,
my heart tight and without history.

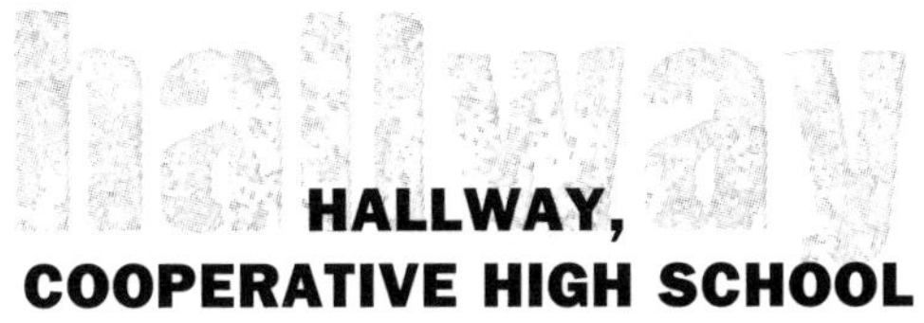

HALLWAY, COOPERATIVE HIGH SCHOOL

That's why nobody
won't talk to nobody
no more, he says.

Jesus did not have to whisper.

FOR DELIVERANCE

This woman I know
wakes to coffee, forgets the paper,
can't bear a prayer,
is obsessed with the *here*, the *there* and the *how*.
And all around her, the wind pushing.

I know she can't be waiting
to turn back to the flash—
the roll from the hip, note of a moan
grazing a chord, hope's shadow.

You can relax, I tell her. See,
the news swims in your soup,
writhes in your coffee,
sticks to your soles,
finger-signs in your sleep,
cums in your bed,
saran wraps itself to your lunch,
is in the legs of a dust mite,
hangs from the arms of a tree,
travels your uterine canal with your bath—

but if your heart is a gas tank
you fill up with clumps
from the grave of the soul of the world,
pain will find you anyhow.

BRUJO NO. 1 FOR THE PAPI CHULO WHO MUST GO

Bad feelings are, of course,
not allowed in the kitchen—
bad medicine hurts
the seeker first.

When loving him off, though,
has all too often been
your remedy of choice,
skip the tostones,
the arroz con gandures.

Cook a bird whose feathers
you've burned off.
Scatter these ashes
on a pungent sauce,
mixed well with herbs—
especially sage,
preferably espantamuerto.

Never mind the salad,
the obligatory aguacate.
You want plain, saltless
calabaza, other
undercooked verduras.

Replace the Spanish olive oil
with American margarine—
served melted, with cilantro
to make it pretty—
and seven drops of olvido oil.

Light a black candle.
The color scares non-believers
who think only white
is for purification.

This is not a night for blades,
but be a ninja
of your own kitchen.
As he sits in the comedor,
move with stealth,
making small talk
with the herb beings
who inhabit your cupboards.
Ask them to disguise
his first few bites.

Serve the meal up
in the kitchen.
Hold the thought of him
you most dislike,
and calling on your abuelitas,
blow your breath
over the plates.

Be polite.
Before his first bite,
apologize for the meal.
You don't know what happened
to you today. Not really.

SANACIÓN, BARRIO

They tell us to drink
and I race out to Mercy Street
with my hands on fire.

I want to break the dam
on the beer tap,
for new scriptures to fly
from some jagged teeth
that can turn rocks
into cypresses.

I want to be alone
with the entire world,
to touch down
on my own photosynthesis,

not care what twitches
on my body,
what old muscle's flexibility
has been lost.

DECLARACIÓN NO. 999 FOR HARMONY

The difference between you and me,
when we walk by that tree on the hillside:
I hear a conga playing inside the wood,
Eddie Palmieri wailing in the leaves.
And it's not that the birds could not
be singing an opera.
There is an opera inside there, too.

BRUJO NO. 28
FOR DRAWING YOUR ANCESTORS

Face it. This here's about loss
and regaining what's been lost.
Call your spirit back.
What is the birthing song you need?
The secret vow?
If your day is a drum, then drum.
The rest is about dancing.

EYES LOOKING

They flit about
unconsciously, she says.
Over the empty
shadowlands.
Breathe.

I lie over my blanket
for our pelvic
bowl pose,
remember the blue
shawl I wrapped
myself in one winter
when my eyes
craved everything
dark beneath the earth.

I remember
the abuelitos
of my life,
how I could lose
myself inside
their eyes,
where I learned to look
differently.

I remember the eyes
of all the brown
people I bury mine in
on the bus to work,

in the streets
of my tiny barrio
turned development
host—the picking
hands lifting pails,
the stockrooms
and factories,
the fortune-talking
lottery lunch
over our barters
of survival.

I pray for these eyes
that give my own
their way of looking,
that give my soul a window
for the air to come in.

MANIFESTO

I sit with poetry,
glad and big.
I am a hungry Buddha,
five times my size.
I step into the temple
of my midnight room.
Sing the cricket
song of night gone.
Light a candle.
The coquí song of dawn
arrives for me.
I am a singer,
loud and strong.
The sky is empty.
The wind sings back.
I bathe in word water
and dream up
flower sounds.
My own skies feel clean.
My heart is good.
I work my words.
I pray my songs.
I sing my work and work
works for me.
I sleep awake.
Awake, I dream.
I apologize for this no more.

NOTES

In Yoruba medicine, medicinal incantations (or *ofo*), most of which use a form of word-play, are used to call on the properties of plants to awaken their healing power. These incantations are addressed to deities or other human beings. Yoruba medicine greatly influenced the practice of spiritism and *santería* in Puerto Rico, as it did other spiritual practices elsewhere in the Caribbean and Latin America.

L'Évolution créatrice, p. 5

L'Évolution créatrice is a 1907 book by French philosopher Henri-Louis Bergson. The book suggests an alternative explanation for Darwin's mechanism of evolution: evolution is brought about by *élan vital*, a "vital impetus" that is humanity's natural creative impulse. The book influenced modernist thinkers and writers like Marcel Proust. The English translation was published in 1911.

Declaración Número Sabe-Quién for a Telling-Off, p. 10

A *declaración* is a statement, testimony, announcement, representation, or declaration. The Spanish in this title, a take-off on the numbered spells that appear elsewhere in the book, means "Statement Number Who-Knows-What."

Brujo No. 7, Against the Noise of Urban Development, p. 11

In Spanish, a *brujo* is a male sorcerer or witch. In Puerto Rico, however, *brujos* are also spells, many of which employ the use of herbs and other organic products as well as prayers or incantations cast to accomplish a specific outcome. *Pa'lante* is a common expression, meaning "onward."*Bachatas* and merengues are two types of music and their corresponding dances.

Sanación No. 11, Mt. Rainier, p. 15

Another take-off on the numbered spells, *sanación* translates to "a healing." Tahoma, or Talol, is the Lushootseed name of Mt. Rainier given by the Puyallup people who, numbering about 4,000, continue to live along the shores of Puget Sound today.

Taíno Is in Me, p. 25

The Taíno are the indigenous people of the island of Borikén, later named Puerto Rico by the Spaniards. A *güiro* is an instrument played in traditional Puerto Rican folkloric music, such as *aguinaldos*. It is made from a long, hollowed gourd; grooves are scored on the playing side, which is scratched with a fork. A *cuatro* is a traditional Puerto Rican string instrument. Some say it is the island's adaptation of the guitar brought in by the Spaniards, though others say it is the Spanish *vihuela* that the Puerto Rican *cuatro* resembles. While the instrument now has five sets of double strings, at one point it only had a set of four, and Puerto Ricans retained its original name.

Abuela, p. 26

Originally an Ojibwa dance (also performed by the Lakota people and other nations), the Women's Jingle Dress dance is a powwow dance style.

Vieques, p. 28

A *jíbaro*, an icon in Puerto Rican folklore, is someone who dwells in a rural area; also known as a *campesino*.

Migration, p. 29

The words preceding each stanza are the numbers one through six in English spelled to represent the sound of each number as it would be pronounced by a native speaker of Spanish. *Nipa,* a regionalism, is loosely translated as "Never mind." *Aspira que te aspira* means "to aspire over again."

For Light, p. 33

Titi, diminutive of *tía*, is "auntie."

Benediction, p. 34

Loíza, a small town located on the northeastern coast of Puerto Rico, is said to be the birthplace of "plena," a folkloric music and dance. Loíza is known for its traditional Taíno and African dishes and art and its *máscaras de vejigantes,* colorful masks made of coconut shells. *Alcapurrias* are fritters made from a mixture of native tubers, plantain, and green bananas that are filled with ground meat or seafood. Huracán is a Taíno deity, as well as the Taíno word for hurricane.

Chucho, p. 35

Chucho is a nickname for the given name Jesús. In Puerto Rico, arepas are round fritters made from a dough of corn or other flour. Sometimes arepas are stuffed with coconut or seafood. An Orisha (also spelled *Orisa* and *Orixa*) is a deity in Yoruba medicine (e.g., Ochún is an Orisha).

Golden Chopsticks, p. 36

Camarones en ajillo con tostones are shrimp in garlic sauce with twice-fried plantains. *Juguito natural* is fruit nectar. A literal translation of *Mira, prieto* would be "Listen here, Black One." In Puerto Rico "black" (*negro, negra*) or "Little Black Person" (negrito, negrita) is a term of affection for all people, despite the color of their skin. *¡Ay, Papi! Mira, papi, cómo me torturas* translates to "Oh, baby! Listen, baby, oh, how you torture me."

Tiene que ser . . . , p. 37

Tiene que ser is the tagline for Goya, a manufacturer of *adobo*, among other things. *Adobo* is a mixture of garlic and onion powders, ground oregano, salt, black pepper, turmeric, and sometimes, cumin and dried citrus zest.

Pasteles, a staple of the Christmas holiday season in Puerto Rico, are similar to tamales in shape, size, and the way they are cooked. While the dough for tamales is made from corn meal, the dough for *pasteles* is made from green bananas and tropical tubers. Though the wrapper in tamales is usually a corn husk, the wrapper in Puerto Rican *pasteles* is always an oiled banana leaf.

Mami, in this case, is the diminutive of "mother." *Asopao* is stew, and *arroz con gandures*, rice with pigeon peas. *Sofrito* is a mixture of sweet peppers, cilantro, *recao*, yellow Spanish onion, garlic, and sometimes annatto or saffron. The mixture is typically prepared fresh and added as a seasoning to most Puerto Rican dishes. *Recao*, a staple seasoning in Puerto Rican cooking, is an herb whose taste is similar to cilantro. Medicinally, the plant is said to calm the spirit and has been used to treat epilepsy. The roots and leaves can be used to stimulate the appetite and improve digestion, as well as to relieve colic, stomach pains, and gas.

Cántaro, p. 39

Pitcher, jug.

Because She Asked, p. 41

A *truya*, also known as a *parranda* or an *asalto navideño*, is a Puerto Rican tradition in which a group of family or friends surprises an unsuspecting, familiar household with festive Christmas folk songs and music (known as *aguinaldos*). Those "receiving" the *truya* open their doors to serve traditional Christmas food and drink, no matter the hour, bringing out their own instruments to share and, traditionally, leaving with those who came to surprise another home. *Truyas* have been known to last until sunrise and beyond.

Pitorro, also known as "ron caña" or "cañita," is an illegal Puerto Rican moonshine drunk typically around the Christmas holidays. *Coquito* is an eggnog-like rum and coconut milk drink popular during the Christmas holidays. *Mondongo* is pork tripe stew.

Loosely, *sereno* is the cool, damp night air, which is thought to make one more vulnerable to disease or malaise. (See Jack Agüero's poem "Sonnet for Naomi Ayala Who Asked Me" in *Sonnets from the Puerto Rican*, Hanging Loose Press, 1996, page 43.)

Bridge Across the Pond, p. 42

To cross the pond, or *cruzar el charco,* is a term referring to travel between Puerto Rico and the United States. It is often used to indicate not just the geographic proximity but the ease (since Puerto Ricans are born into U.S. citizenship) with which we travel between island and mainland. For arepas, see the poem "Chucho." *El viento está jodío* translates to "the wind is fucked up."

Carmen Inés Goes to the Botánica, p. 44

A *botánica* is a store that sells folk medicine (these may be herbs or herbal remedies), candles, statues, and amulets. *Botánicas* often bring together an area's spiritual community and provide services such as card-reading, the throwing of shells or bones, and recipes for spells. An *escapulario* is a small piece of square cloth bearing a representation of a religious image that devotees wear under their clothing like an amulet. *Ay, bendito* is a popular regionalism, denoting supplication, which is akin to a request for mercy. An *imán* is a lodestone.

One Season, p. 47

Considered the center point in Yoruba theogony, Changó (also spelled Sango, Shango, and Xangô) is one of the most popular Orishas in Yoruba medicine; he is the Sky Father, god of thunder and lightning. In Puerto Rico's *santería* practice, Changó is also venerated as Santa Barbara (the traditional colonial disguise in Catholicism for this deity). For *recao*, see "Tiene que ser. . . ."

Turtle Country, p. 57

The people of many first nations, such as the Ojibwa/Anishinabe and the Iroquois, refer to North America as Turtle Island. The name comes from a creation story that varies from nation to nation: In essence, a female deity, the first woman, fell from the sky and needed firm ground to stand upon. The animals tried to make a place for her to land, and, after trying to find other solutions, Turtle offered her back, on which the world was formed.

Lontananza, p. 64

In a painting, *lontananza* is the background.

Brujo No. 1 for the Papi Chulo Who Must Go, p. 69

Espantamuerto is a plant whose leaves and stems are cooked in water and used in *despojos* (cleansing baths) to remove evil spirits, an unhealthy attachment to the living by those who have passed on, as well as to chase away bad spells. *Verduras* are vegetables; however, in Puerto Rico, *verduras* refers to tubers, such as *yuca*, and tree vegetables, such as breadfruit. *Olvido* oil is an anointing oil used to intentionally forget someone or something.

Manifesto, p. 76

The *coquí*, a small arboreal frog native to Puerto Rico, is one of the national symbols of the island. Its song has come to define Puerto Ricans' connection to the land and their uniqueness as a people.

PERMISSIONS AND SOURCE ACKNOWLEDGMENTS

My thanks to the editors of the following publications, and the curators at the venues, in which these poems first appeared, sometimes in slightly different form.

Hanging Loose Magazine. "Golden Chopsticks"

The Hostos Review/Revista Hostoniana. "Lineage," which appeared as "I Remember."

Saranac Review. "Trasnocharse" and "No. 13, for Remembering," which appeared as "13th Street."

MARGIN: Exploring Modern Magical Realism. "Puerto Rico," which appeared as "Puerto Pobre."

Terra Incognita: A Bilingual Journal of Literature, Art & Commentary. "Consejo No. 13, Given by an Otherwise Ill-Willed Papi Chulo" and "Brujo No. 1 for the Papi Chulo Who Must Go."

Letras (Center for Puerto Rican Studies)."Brujo No. 7, Against the Noise of Urban Development," "Brujo No. 39, for Ease," "Migration," and "Declaración No. 999."

Red River Review. "Clean Slate," which appeared as "When You Left."

Anomalous."In Winter."

The Poet's Cookbook: Recipes from Germany and Poems by 33 American Poets with German Translations. "Two Tamales."

Folger Shakespeare Library, O.B. Hardison Poetry Series broadside. "Manifesto."

Hamiltonian Gallery, *Call & Response* exhibit. "Eyes Looking."

Inter-American Development Bank Gallery, *Nuestras Voces, Nuestras Imágenes* exhibit. "Lineage," which appeared in English as "I Remember" and in Spanish as "Recuerdo."